THE FISH BOOK

INTRODUCING TROPICAL FISH

Written by CYNTHIA OVERBECK
Illustrated by SHARON LERNER

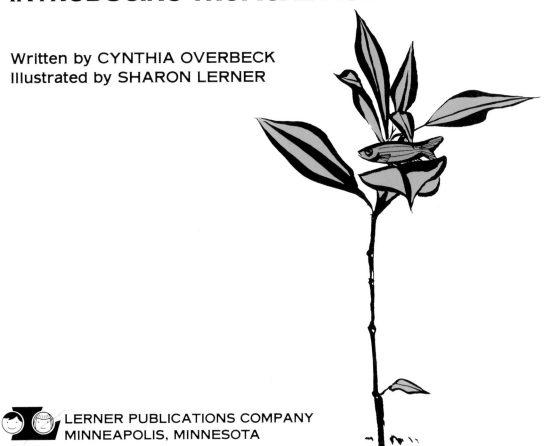

LERNER PUBLICATIONS COMPANY
MINNEAPOLIS, MINNESOTA

LIBRARY OF CONGRESS CATALOGING IN PUBLICATION DATA

Overbeck, Cynthia.
The fish book.

(An Early Nature Picture Book)
SUMMARY: Introduces twelve fish, both fresh and salt-
water, that are native to the tropics.

1. Fishes — Tropics — Pictorial works — Juvenile literature.
2. Aquarium fishes — Pictorial works — Juvenile literature.
[1. Tropical fish. 2. Fishes] I. Lerner, Sharon. II. Title.

QL637.5.O93 1978   597'.09201'3   78-7205
ISBN 0-8225-1110-X

AN EARLY NATURE PICTURE BOOK

International Standard Book Number: 0-8225-1110-X
Library of Congress Catalog Card Number: 78-7205

1 2 3 4 5 6 7 8 9 10 85 84 83 82 81 80 79 78

CONTENTS

In the waters of the world live thousands of different kinds of fish. Many of the world's most colorful and interesting fish live in the **tropics.** The tropics are the parts of the earth near the equator. There the weather and the water are always warm. Some tropical fish live in the salty waters of the oceans. Others live in the fresh waters of lakes, rivers, or ponds.

You may not get a chance to travel to the faraway rivers and oceans where these beautiful fish live. But perhaps you will see some of them at a pet store or a zoo. In this book are some of the fish that you might see.

BETTA

The betta (BET-uh) is a fierce little fish from the fresh waters of Thailand (Siam). Male bettas will fight each other whenever they get the chance. For this reason, bettas are also called **Siamese fighting fish.**

But male bettas are not always so fierce. In fact, they are very good parents. When a male and a female betta are ready to have a family, the male builds a **bubble nest.** He blows many tiny bubbles that stick together to make a nest. After the female betta lays her eggs, the male picks them up in his mouth. He puts the eggs in the nest and watches over them until they hatch.

KISSING GOURAMI

The kissing gourami (gu-RAH-mee) is a freshwater fish that comes from Indonesia. There are many other kinds of gouramis. Some of them are very colorful and bright. Kissing gouramis are not as colorful. But they are interesting to watch. They often touch each other's thick lips, as if they are kissing. Nobody is quite sure why they do this. What looks like a kiss may really be a way of trying to start a fight!

ANGELFISH

The angelfish has beautiful fins that look like angel wings. Its arrow-shaped body is very thin. Such a thin body is just right for slipping between rocks and weeds under the water. At home in the rivers of South America, the shy little angelfish likes to hide in just such places.

The angelfish's black stripes also help to hide it from its enemies. Among the waving river plants and moving shadows, enemies find it hard to see the outline of this fish's body. This is because the stripes break up the outline. The stripe across the angelfish's eye also makes the eye hard to see.

EMPEROR ANGELFISH

Other kinds of angelfish live in salt water. This emperor angelfish lives in the Pacific Ocean. It is one of the most beautiful fish in the sea. The colors and patterns of this fish's body change almost completely during its lifetime. When the fish is young, its body is a deep blue color. It has bright white stripes that make a pattern of circles. As an adult, the emperor angelfish looks very different. Its stripes change their pattern. Its body becomes a bright combination of golden yellow and bold blue stripes.

12

COMET GOLDFISH

The goldfish is not a true tropical fish. It can live in cool ponds as well as in warm tropical ones. Goldfish were first kept by the Chinese over a thousand years ago. Today, they are found all over the world.

The fish in the picture is a comet goldfish. There are many other kinds of goldfish as well. Some of them have very fancy fins. Like other fish, goldfish use their fins and tails to steer through the water. Most fish have seven fins. Besides a tail fin, a fish has one fin on its back and three fins along its stomach. It also has one fin on each side of its body near its head. You can only see five of this fish's fins.

BLEEDING HEART TETRA

The pretty little tetra is a freshwater fish from Central and South America. Tetras can be many colors. The bleeding heart tetra has a bright red spot on its side that looks like a heart.

The tetra is one fish that is not a very good parent. Some fish, like the angelfish, lay their eggs carefully on a reed and watch over them. Others, like the betta, build nests to protect their eggs. But tetras just scatter their eggs everywhere. Then they swim away. When the baby fish, or **fry**, are born, they are on their own.

16

FOUR-EYED BUTTERFLY FISH

The four-eyed butterfly fish seems to have eyes on both ends of its body! But the "eye" near its tail is really just a spot of color. Nature gave this fish big spots on its body to trick its enemies.

The butterfly fish lives among sea plants and corals in the Caribbean Sea. There, the light often plays tricks. The butterfly fish's enemies cannot see its real eye very well because it has a black stripe through it. They see only the huge "eye" near its tail. They think that they are staring right into the eye of a very big fish. That scares them away in a hurry!

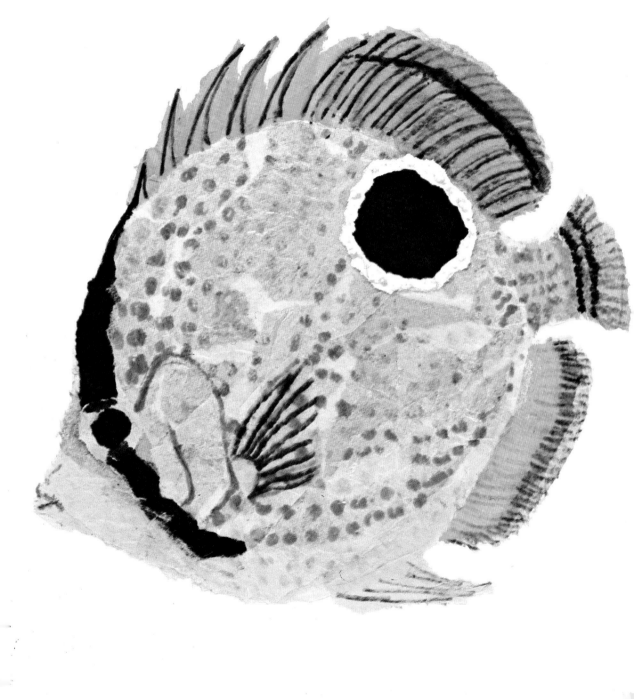

LEOPARD CATFISH

The funny little leopard catfish has "whiskers" that look almost like those of a cat. These "whiskers" are called **barbels.** In the rivers of South America, the catfish uses its barbels to feel for objects in the water. The little fish swims along the muddy river bottom, searching for scraps of food.

The leopard catfish has a pattern of dark spots on its body that look like a leopard's markings. Another name for this fish is the **leopard corydora** (kuh-RID-uh-ruh).

VEILTAIL GUPPY

Guppies are hardy, active little freshwater fish. They come from the waters of South America and the West Indies. Most female guppies are plain and grey. But males, like this veiltail, are very beautiful. Fancy male guppies can have any one of 12 different fin shapes, as well as many beautiful colors.

Guppies are one kind of fish whose babies are born live. The female guppy does not lay her eggs to hatch in a nest or on a reed. Instead, her eggs hatch inside her body. Then the tiny fry are born alive, wiggling and squirming.

CLOWN FISH

The clown fish is a funny little character. With its bright orange and white stripes, it seems to be dressed up for the circus!

Clown fish live in the Indian and Pacific oceans. They share the water with sea anemones (uh-NEM-uh-neez), strange animals that look like underwater flowers. Anemones have long arms called **tentacles.** The tentacles carry a poison that kills many fish but does not hurt the clown fish. The clown fish has learned to live among the anemone's tentacles. There it is safe from bigger fish. Meanwhile, the anemone eats other fish that follow its little friend too close to its deadly tentacles.

TOPSAIL PLATY

The topsail platy (PLAD-ee) is one of the most beautiful of the freshwater tropical fish. Its home is in the waters of Mexico. Platies are a plain greyish color until they are about nine months old. Then they become very colorful.

There are many kinds of platies. The one in the picture is called a **topsail variatus** (ver-ee-AHD-us) **platy.** The beautiful high fin on its back looks like a brightly colored gold sail.

Like the guppy's babies, the platy's fry are born alive. A mother platy can give birth to several dozen babies at once!

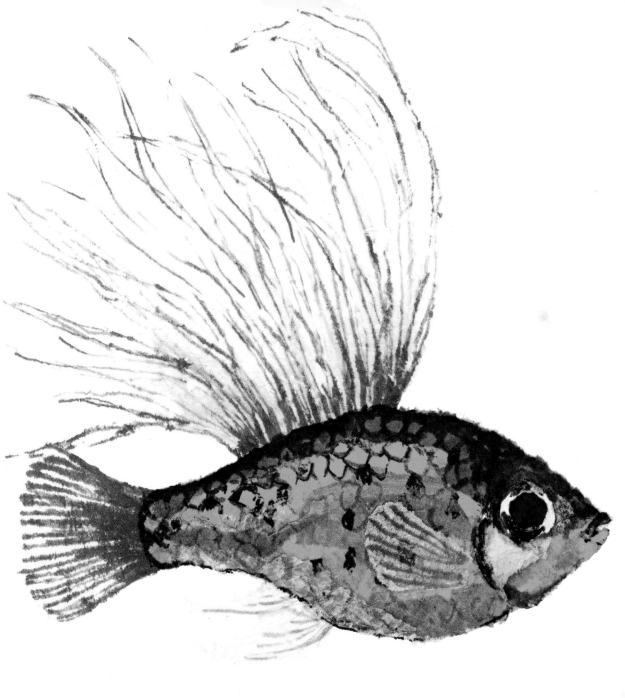

LIONFISH

The lionfish is a fearsome looking creature! Its spines and long, waving fins look frightening when they are spread out around the fish's body. And they can be as dangerous as they look. The first 11 spines on the lionfish's back are poisonous. They can give a painful sting to a person or to another fish. But the lionfish only uses its spines to protect itself from enemies in its home in the Indo-Pacific Ocean.

Because it looks so frightening, this fish is also called the **dragonfish.**

28

HOW MANY KINDS OF FISH?

In this book you have read about 12 different kinds of tropical fish. But there are hundreds more, from both the fresh waters and the salty oceans of the tropics. They are interesting to learn about as well as lovely

to watch. Their habits are as unusual as their beautiful colors and fancy fin shapes. Their number is endless. So the next time you visit a pet store or aquarium, see how many different kinds of tropical fish you can discover!

Children are curious about the world around them. They enjoy learning about the plants and animals in their environment—about the vegetables that grow in the garden and the bright butterflies that appear each spring. In these books, simple language and colorful illustrations make the natural world meaningful to young readers. The books may even inspire children to plant gardens, to raise tropical fish, or to start collections of their own.

THE BUTTERFLY BOOK
THE FISH BOOK
THE FLOWER BOOK
THE FRUIT BOOK
THE LEAF BOOK
THE VEGETABLE BOOK

Young readers will also want to see these Art Concept books:

ORANGE IS A COLOR
SQUARE IS A SHAPE
STRAIGHT IS A LINE